KU-772-293

# THE LITTLE BOOK OF

*Christmas Joys*

H. Jackson Brown, Jr.,
Rosemary Brown, and Kathy Peel

RUTLEDGE HILL PRESS ● Nashville, Tennessee

©1994 by H. Jackson Brown, Jr.
All rights reserved. Written permission must be secured from the publisher to use or
reproduce any part of this book, except for brief quotations in critical reviews or articles.

Published in Nashville, Tennessee, by Rutledge Hill Press, Inc.,
211 Seventh Avenue North, Nashville, Tennessee 37219, U.S.A.
Distributed by Verulam Publishing Ltd., 1522 Park Street Lane,
Park Street, St. Albans, Herts. AL2 2AU.

Typography by D&T/Bailey Typesetting, Inc., Nashville, Tennessee
Design by Bruce Gore, Gore Studio, Inc.

**Library of Congress Cataloging-in-Publication Data**

Brown, H. Jackson, 1940–
    The little book of Christmas joys / by H. Jackson Brown, Jr.
Rosemary Brown, Kathy Peel.
        p.    cm.
    ISBN 1–55853–310–9 (pbk.)
    1. Christmas.    I. Brown, Rosemary, 1945–    .    II. Peel, Kathy,
1951–    .    III. Title.
GT4985.B726      1994
394.2'.663—dc20                    Printed by Vaughan Printing                    94-30410
                                                                                                            CIP

Printed in the United States of America
3 4 5 6 7 8 9 — 98 97 96 95 94

# Introduction

On a frosty December evening, my wife, Rosemary, and I and our friends the Peels were enjoying mugs of steaming spiced cider while watching the Christmas holiday classic, *It's a Wonderful Life*. A softly crackling fire silhouetted the Christmas stockings hanging from the mantelpiece as we savoured every familiar line until the movie reached its joyful ending. For fifteen years, hot cider, good friends, and *It's a Wonderful Life* have been the traditional ways my family has welcomed the Christmas season.

As I tossed another log on the fire, the four of us reminisced about the cherished Christmas traditions our families had maintained and the new ones we had lovingly created. We marvelled at the power of Christmas traditions and the comfort and continuity they bring to us each year.

We decided to pool our experiences into a collection of familiar and unique ways that our families and others have learned to *make it*

*Christmas*. And so, there in front of a crackling Christmas fire, the idea for *The Little Book of Christmas Joys* was formed.

It is the excitement and anticipation of favourite Christmas traditions that help make this the most joyful time of the year. Even a small child senses something wonderful is about to happen when the loft ladder is pulled down, dark recesses of cupboards are explored, and the search begins for Christmas decorations that have been hibernating since last year. Our homes take on a distinctive fragrance as the halls are decked with fresh greenery and kitchens yield themselves to enthusiastic efforts and friendly disorder. Refrains from familiar carols fill the air with joy to the world as families are reunited and old friends embraced. Hope is renewed for peace on earth as we remember a baby born two thousand years ago.

It is our hope that *The Little Book of Christmas Joys* will bring an extra measure of joy to your Christmas season. You might discover, as we did, that joy almost always comes as a result of giving—giving gifts, giving hugs, giving help, giving a second chance, giving encouragement, and giving of ourselves.

Perhaps our suggestions will remind you of some old traditions you need to revive or some fresh new ideas you might want to try. But remember, the most treasured Christmas traditions develop slowly. Like the roasting holiday turkey, there's no need to hurry them along. So relax and let yourself enjoy the season of seasons.

From our homes to yours, we wish you the merriest and most joyful holiday ever. And may the blessing of Christmas bring hope, love, and joy to each day of your New Year.

H. J. B.
Tall Pine Lodge
Fernvale, Tennessee

## Other books by H. Jackson Brown, Jr.

*A Father's Book of Wisdom*
*P.S. I Love You*
*Life's Little Instruction Book*
*Live and Learn and Pass It On*
*Life's Little Instruction Book, Volume II*

1 ◆ Be the first to wish everyone you meet a Merry Christmas.

2 ◆ Buy a pair of red flannel pajamas that you wear only on Christmas Eve.

3 ◆ Take the family to see a small town Christmas parade.

4 ◆ Don't count calories from December 15th to January 2nd.

5 ◆ Never select a Christmas tree after dark.

6 ◆ Mend a broken relationship with a friend or relative during the holidays.

7 ◆ Take a basket of Christmas goodies to a notoriously grumpy neighbour.

8 ◆ Be nice to sales personnel. They're often wearier than you are.

9 ◆ Don't schedule yourself too tightly during the season. Before making an appointment, ask yourself, "Can this wait until after Christmas?"

10 ◆ Take a Christmas family photograph each year in the same spot, such as by a favourite tree in your garden. In years to come, you'll have a wonderful record of the growth of your family, as well as of the growth of the tree.

11 ◆ Find out what's on everyone's Christmas wish list early in the autumn.

12 ◆ Make an effort to attend every Christmas party you're invited to, even if you can stay only a few minutes.

13 ◆ Place your children's stuffed animals under the Christmas tree as a welcoming committee for Santa.

14 ◆ Adopt a needy family this Christmas. Let members of your family buy a present for the person closest to their own age.

15 ◆ Fill your house with the holiday fragrance of cloves, orange peel, and cinnamon sticks simmering on the kitchen stove.

16 ◆ Don't despair if you are short of cash. Be creative. Looking back, you'll discover that the Christmases when you had the least money were the ones that left you with the best memories.

17 ◆ Ask your mother to send you the Christmas stocking you used when you were a kid and a couple of old family Christmas photos.

18 ◆ Let go of a problem you can't solve. Enjoy the season.

19 ◆ Hang a favourite Christmas tree ornament from your car's rear-view mirror.

20 ◆ Sprinkle red and green confetti in your Christmas card envelopes.

21 ◆ Introduce a child to the wonders of snowflakes. Chill a dark sheet of paper and then examine the flakes with a magnifying glass.

22 ◆ Bake Christmas goodies while a Johnny Mathis Christmas album plays in the background.

23 ◆ Take a few minutes each month during the year to jot down your family's news. This will make writing your Christmas letter a lot easier.

24 ◆ Take a basket of Christmas goodies to your local fire and police stations.

25 ◆ Wear a smile and a Santa hat when you walk through the shopping precinct.

26 ◆ Early in December ask a camera store clerk to check your camera's battery.

27 ◆ If your child gives you a handmade gift, convince him it's your favourite gift of all.

28 ◆ If you bake a variety of Christmas goodies in advance, be sure to wrap each type separately to keep the flavours and textures distinct.

29 ◆ Be considerate of your in-laws' special Christmas traditions.

30 ◆ Purchase a special Christmas sweater and wear it often.

31 ◆ Choose a Christmas tree that's a little too big for the room.

32 ◆ Tie a wreath with a big, red bow to the grill of your car.

## (33) ◆ *Scotch Shortbread*

These shortbread biscuits make a wonderful gift for friends. But you may need to hide them to keep family members from devouring the biscuits before you can give them away.

---

**Yield: 1 cake    Oven: 170°C/325°F or Gas Mark 2**

---

125g plain flour                     50g rice flour/ground rice
125g butter                          50g castor sugar

Cream butter and sugar until smooth. Mix in ground rice and flour, adding a little at a time. When all the flour is added, knead into a smooth dough. Roll out lightly on a floured board and form into a ½-inch-thick circle. Crimp the edges, prick lightly all over, and mark into wedges. Place on non-stick baking sheet and bake in a slow oven for 1 hour, or until lightly brown. Cool on a wire rack and when completely cold, dust with castor sugar. If desired cut into narrow wedge-shaped pieces.

34 ◆ Have a special place to display the Christmas card from the farthest distance away.

35 ◆ Organize a neighbourhood safari dinner. Have appetizers at one home, the main course at another, and dessert at a third.

36 ◆ Try at least one new recipe and one new decorating idea.

37 ◆ Start working on a Christmas-themed jigsaw puzzle the first of December. Try to have it finished by Christmas Eve.

38 ◆ Take a house-bound person a scrumptious Christmas dinner.

39 ◆ Rent a Santa Claus suit. Slip it on during your lunch hour and hand out sweets to everyone in the office.

40 ◆ Hire students to help with your Christmas entertaining. They can help serve, clean up before and after the party, and perform any number of odd jobs.

41 ◆ If you are short on space, set up a card table and cover it with a plaid tablecloth that reaches to the floor. Tuck all your gift-wrapping supplies under the table.

42 ◆ Take your family to a live performance of *The Nutcracker Suite*.

43 ◆ Take your family to a church choir's performance of Handel's *Messiah*.

44 ◆ Before going to bed on Christmas Eve, read by candlelight about the birth of Jesus in Luke, chapter 2. Then join hands with your family and sing "Silent Night".

45 ◆ Personalize your Christmas cards with a short hand-written note.

46 ◆ Don't forget our feathered friends during the holidays. Spread peanut butter on pine cones, then roll them in bird seed, and hang them on a tree near your kitchen window.

47 ◆ Tie jingle bells on your kid's shoelaces.

48. When you think you have enough lights on your tree, add two more strings.

49 ◆ Throw restraint to the wind. Christmas is the one time of year when bigger is better and gaudy is good.

50 ◆ Don't wait until Christmas Eve to wrap gifts. Wrap them as you purchase them.

51 ◆ Give a young member of your family the honour of placing the star or angel on top of the tree.

52 ◆ When sending a perishable food gift, schedule the delivery date when you know the recipient will be at home or at work to receive it.

53 ◆ Go caroling.

54 ◆ Avoid backtracking when doing your Christmas shopping. Be sure you've finished in one department or store before you move on to the next.

55 ◆ Instead of the usual bedtime stories, read to your children about the Christmas customs in other countries.

56 ◆ Check for loose or burned-out bulbs *before* you put the strings of lights on the tree.

57 ◆ Buy more Sellotape, wrapping paper, and enclosure cards than you think you'll need.

58 ◆ Lists help you get organized. Sit down on a Sunday afternoon in November and make lists of gifts you want to give, supplies you need to purchase, Christmas goodies you will prepare, and people you would like to entertain during the Christmas season.

59 ◆ Deliver delicious mince pies to your neighbours to enjoy on Christmas morning.

60 ◆ Never write the word *Christmas* as *Xmas.*

61 ◆ Enjoy a couple of meals illuminated only by the Christmas tree.

62 ◆ Recycle. Instead of throwing away wrinkled ribbon, run it through a curling iron to straighten it out. Use wrinkled wrapping paper as packing material.

## 63 ◆ *Rosemary's Cranberry Salad*

Even if it's not your turn to cook the Christmas dinner, you'll probably want to make this treat just to serve with turkey sandwiches. To make relish instead of set salad, leave out the unflavoured gelatine and orange juice.

---

**Yield: 16 to 20 servings**

---

450g cranberries
4 oranges, one unpeeled
1 474g can crushed pineapple
   in juice

450g sugar
120ml orange juice
3 sachets unflavoured gelatine
225g pecan nuts

Wash and sort the cranberries. Peel all but one orange and cut up all of the oranges. In a blender or food processor blend the cranberries and oranges. Add the drained pineapple, reserving the juice. Stir in the sugar and mix well. In a small saucepan combine the reserved pineapple juice and orange juice. Sprinkle the gelatine on top and stir. Heat until the gelatine is completely dissolved. Add the gelatine to the fruit mixture. Fold in the nuts. Pour into a greased 3-litre mould. Chill until set. Turn out on to a serving dish and serve with mayonnaise.

64 ◆ If you're feeling overwhelmed, break down big projects into manageable tasks. For example, divide the number of Christmas cards you want to send by ten, and address one-tenth of the list each day for ten days.

65 ◆ During the year, collect inexpensive antique table napkins at flea markets and car boot sales. Use them to line baskets of Christmas goodies.

66 ◆ Take pictures after you've finished decorating your home. Not only will they be fun to look at later on, but you will have a visual reminder to help you decorate next year.

67 ◆ Try to finish your Christmas shopping by December 10.

68 ◆ Try to have all Christmas packages posted by December 12.

69 ◆ Before going to bed every night of the Christmas season, ask yourself, "Whose life did I make brighter today?"

70 ◆ Volunteer as a family to work in a soup kitchen or homeless shelter during the holidays.

71 ◆ Remind newlyweds to save an item from their wedding ceremony to use as a treasured Christmas ornament.

72 ◆ Send a Christmas basket to a student the first of December. Include a Christmas music cassette or CD, decorations for the dorm room, Christmas cards, stamps, and a red pen.

73 ◆ Remember the three rules for reducing holiday hassles: (1) Plan ahead; (2) Begin early; (3) Keep it simple.

74 ◆ Don't give anyone a fruitcake.

75 ◆ Don't give a child underwear.

76 ◆ Don't give your spouse a bathroom scale.

77 ◆ Call a nursing home and get the names of five people who don't often receive mail. Send each one a beautiful Christmas card. Sign it, "from Santa".

78 ◆ Tip someone who doesn't expect it.

79 ◆ Wait until Christmas morning to place the infant Jesus in your Nativity scene.

80 ◆ Remember that the best solution for holiday blues is to do something special for someone else.

81 ◆ Tell your children about Christmas when you were their age.

82 ◆ Wear a colourful Christmas tie to holiday parties.

83 ◆ Wear outrageous Christmas socks.

84 ◆ Give new friends who have just moved to town a newspaper subscription from their hometown.

85 ◆ Buy Christmas mugs for everyone in the family.

85 a Everyone should have a pair of Christmas earrings or badge

86 ◆ Sleep under a homemade quilt on Christmas Eve.

87 ◆ Watch *It's a Wonderful Life*.

88 ◆ Watch Albert Finney in *Scrooge*.

89 ◆ Listen to "A Service of Nine Lessons and Carols" from Kings College Chapel, Cambridge, on Christmas Eve day.

90 ◆ Offer to run Christmas errands for an elderly friend or relative.

91 ◆ Give someone with failing eyesight the large-print edition of a classic book.

92 ◆ Cut off the fronts of attractive Christmas cards to use as gift tags.

93 ◆ Record a cheerful Christmas greeting for your answering machine.

94 ◆ Attend a Christmas Eve candlelight or watch night service with your family.

95 ◆ Remember your milkman, postman, bin men, and delivery people with a gift of cash.

96 ◆ Make snow angels.

97 ◆ Learn to say "Merry Christmas" in several languages.

98 ◆ Design and post a homemade Christmas card to each member of the family.

99 ◆ Attend a church Christmas bazaar. Buy something whether you need it or not.

100 ◆ Get out old games—Monopoly, draughts, Scrabble, and Trivial Pursuits—and have an ongoing family tournament during December.

101 ◆ Begin a family Christmas journal. Write down memories your family shares: events you attend, presents you give and receive, and the inevitable crises that occur.

102 ◆ Buy a hot glue gun to help in creating Christmas decorations.

103 ◆ Give an anonymous gift of money to someone who has been laid off.

104 ◆ Start a special collection for each of your children, adding one item each Christmas.

105 ◆ Ask for a gift box for each gift you buy.

106 ◆ Help an elderly neighbour decorate his or her home.

107 ◆ Curl up before an open fire with someone you love.

108 ◆ Remember that the more a toy costs, the more likely kids will want to play with the box it came in.

109 ◆ Never refuse a Christmas dessert.

110 ◆ Stock up on staples and nonperishable foods you'll need for the holidays before the crowds get heavy at the supermarket.

111 ◆ On Christmas morning, phone some relatives who live far away and wish them a Merry Christmas.

112 ◆ Help your children bake Christmas mince pies to give to teachers, coaches, and school bus drivers.

113 ◆ Display prominently the Christmas artwork your child brings home from school.

114 ◆ If there's a model train in the loft or hidden in a cupboard, get it out and set it up under the tree.

## 115 ◆ Santa's Thumbprint Biscuits

Even a very young cook can have a "hands-on" experience making thumbprints in these delicious biscuits.

---

**Yield: about 3 dozen biscuits   Oven: 190°C/375°F or Gas Mark 5**

---

| | |
|---|---|
| 225g butter | 45g S.R. flour |
| 150g sugar | 45ml poppy seeds |
| 2 egg yolks | Blackcurrant or strawberry jam |
| 5ml vanilla essence | White decorator's icing |

In a large bowl cream the butter with an electric mixer at medium speed. Add the sugar, beating until light and fluffy. Beat in the egg yolks and vanilla. Gradually beat in the flour and poppy seeds. Wrap the dough in plastic wrap. Refrigerate for 1 to 2 hours, until chilled.

Shape the dough into 1-inch balls. Place on non-stick baking trays, about 2 inches apart. Press the centre of each biscuit with a thumb to form indentations. Bake for 12 to 14 minutes, or until lightly browned. Remove to wire racks to cool. Press the indentations again while the biscuits are still warm. Just before serving, spoon jam into the indentations and decorate with icing. Store in an airtight container.

116 ◆ Videotape family members recalling their favourite Christmas memories.

117 ◆ Unplug the Christmas lights before going to bed or leaving your house.

118 ◆ At least once in your life, visit London and go to a major West End Christmas pantomime, see the giant Christmas tree in Trafalgar Square, and enjoy the spectacular Christmas lights in Regent Street.

119 ◆ Buy a big wall calendar in December. Ask family members to write down their activities, so there won't be any mix-ups.

120 ◆ Never give your credit card number over the phone unless you initiated the call.

121 ◆ Relax with your family Christmas afternoon by looking at photos and videos from past Christmases.

122 ◆ Listen to the Barking Dogs "sing" "Jingle Bells". Once.

123 ◆ Before you buy any item over £25, check into the store's return policy.

124 ◆ Take a batch of Christmas goodies to the office for your co-workers to enjoy.

125 ◆ Put something Christmasy in every room of your home.

126 ◆ Remember that Christmas carols never sound better than when you sing them in church.

127 ◆ Take photos of your child's Christmas programme. Have extra prints made for parents who could not attend.

128 ◆ End an evening with family and close friends by forming a circle, holding hands, and singing a favourite carol.

129 ◆ When a family member looks really stressed out, give them a big hug.

130 ◆ Take the family out to eat at the same restaurant every year before picking out and bringing home the Christmas tree.

131 ◆ Don't shop during peak hours. Avoid lunchtime and Saturdays; early mornings and evenings are best.

132 ◆ Don't wait until 1:30 A.M. Christmas morning to start putting together "Some Assembly Required" toys.

133 ◆ If you enjoy cooking, bake double batches of Christmas goodies for your friends who might be too busy to cook.

134 ◆ Enjoy Christmas music in your home, office, and car to keep you in the spirit of the season.

135 ◆ When you don't know what to give, give a book. Inscribe it with your name, the occasion, and the date.

136 ◆ Sometime during the Christmas season, thumb through the toy section of an old Freeman's catalogue.

137 ◆ Fill a basket with photos from past Christmases. Put it in a prominent spot.

138 ◆ Buy only approved weatherproof lights and extension cables for outside use. Wrap the connection with plastic electrical tape.

139 ◆ Whistle "Walking in a Winter Wonderland" in the shower.

140 ◆ Organize a neighbourhood garden decorating contest with the winner receiving a plate of goodies from the losers.

141 ◆ Never set a candle on a counter underneath a cabinet or a shelf. Heat rises and can create a fire hazard.

142 ◆ Create a homemade sledge from a large appliance box. Then look for the biggest hill you can find.

143 ◆ Be creative with gift wrapping. Use old maps, the funny papers, posters, the yellow pages.

144 ◆ Consider buying your Christmas tree from the Boy Scouts or a voluntary organisation's tree sale.

145 ◆ Don't forget that you will get more joy from the gifts you give than from the ones you receive.

146 ◆ Ask your local post office for its recommended posting deadline dates for packages and letters.

147 ◆ Don't send Christmas cash in the post.

148 ◆ Some time during the Christmas season, go through your wardrobes and box up clothing you haven't worn in two years. Give away items that are still in good condition.

149 ◆ Never put away anything that's broken after the holidays, thinking, "I'll get it fixed before I need to use it again next year." Get it fixed now.

150 ◆ When choosing a Christmas tree, pick it up, bounce it on its trunk, then run your hand along a branch. A fresh tree should not drop more than a few needles.

151 ◆ Record names and addresses in your address book as you receive Christmas cards—before you throw away the envelopes.

152 ◆ When you're with a child and see a blinking red light in the sky, ask her, "Do you think that could be Rudolph?"

153 ◆ Allow extra time to navigate through Christmas traffic.

154 ◆ The week before Christmas, talk with
your children about the first Christmas
and how the birth of Jesus has affected
the world.

155 ◆ Offer refreshments to carolers when
they come to your door.

156 ◆ Take along your address book when
Christmas shopping so that you can
send presents directly from the store.

157. ◆ Create a special Christmas morning breakfast menu and serve it every year.

158. ◆ Save a copy of your children's letters to Santa. Put them in a scrapbook to enjoy for years to come.

159. ◆ If your parents live far away, videotape your family decorating the tree and your home and send the video for them to enjoy on Christmas Day.

160 ◆ Take the initiative. Don't wait for someone else to spread Christmas joy.

161 ◆ Take turns opening presents on Christmas morning. When the gift is an article of clothing, it's always fun to ask the recipient to model it.

162 ◆ Arrange for a florist to deliver a Christmas arrangement to a favourite long-distance relative or friend.

(163) ◆ Throughout the Christmas season, give your family the gift of a sweet disposition.

164 ◆ Help your child make red and green paper chains from a packet. Hang them all over her bedroom.

165 ◆ Tie a red plaid bow on your pet's collar.

166 ◆ Try the Swedish custom of writing a short, lighthearted poem on your gift card that half reveals the contents of the package.

167 ◆ Reserve a night for the entire family to make homemade ornaments for your tree.

168 ◆ If a Christmas party requires a tuxedo, wear a sprig of holly as a button hole.

169 ◆ Stock your freezer with meals for the holidays by doubling or tripling recipes for spaghetti sauce, casseroles, and other foods that freeze well.

170 ◆ Make sure that salespeople tear up the carbons of your charge-card purchases.

171 ◆ Order well in advance the special foods you will need for Christmas entertaining.

172 ◆ Along with the gifts, be sure to give children the assurance that they are loved and cherished.

173 ◆ Set aside some time at the beginning of the Christmas season to help your children plan their gift-giving lists.

174 ◆ Give your place in the gift-wrapping line to someone who looks as if she has had a hard day.

175 ◆ As hectic as the season is, try to keep up with your regular fitness routine.

176 ◆ When attending Christmas parties, don't arrive earlier than you were invited, and don't be the last to leave.

177 ◆ Wrap your child's bedroom door with pretty gift paper to transform it into a giant package.

178 ◆ Invite a friend who doesn't have a church home to a special service at your church.

179 ◆ Ask the price of custom gift wrapping *before* you leave the gift to be wrapped. It's often very expensive.

180 ◆ Offer to baby-sit for new parents to give them a chance to do some shopping.

181 ◆ When decorating the tree, nestle photos of past Christmas trees in the branches.

182 ◆ Compliment at least three people every day in December. This is a gift that's always appreciated.

183 ◆ Tape Christmas cards around a doorway so that you can enjoy them each time you walk into the room.

184 ◆ Take some time out to sit in a department store and watch youngsters having their pictures made with Santa.

185 ◆ Remember the fairy lights your parents used to decorate Christmas trees when you were young? They are available again. Buy a couple of strings for old time's sake.

186 ◆ Don't forget the ornament hooks.

187 ◆ Don't forget the extension cables.

188 ◆ Don't forget the brandy and white sauce.

189 ◆ To help it stay fresh, saw an inch off the bottom of your Christmas tree before placing it in the stand. Check the water level every day.

190 ◆ Give your Christmas tree a second life by having it ground into garden mulch.

191 ◆ Include a family photo with Christmas cards sent to relatives and friends you don't see often.

192 ◆ Let your child decorate a small Christmas tree just the way he likes it for his bedroom.

193 ◆ Don't leave packages in plain view when you park your car. Lock them in the boot.

194 ◆ When older children come home for Christmas, remember that they need some privacy and breathing space.

195 ◆ Let the youngest and oldest family members pass out the presents.

196 ◆ Start a collection of Christmas biscuit cutters.

197 ◆ Refuse to let heavy traffic and long queues dampen your Christmas spirit.

198 ◆ Wear a Christmas apron while cooking in the kitchen during December.

199 ◆ Store Christmas candles in a cool, dry place. Never put them next to linens; the dye may fade onto the fabric.

200 ◆ After attending a holiday party, make sure you phone or write to the host to say thank you for a wonderful time.

201 ◆ Go to a Christmas pantomime at a local theatre.

202 ◆ Never give a gift that's not nicely wrapped.

203 ◆ Give a donation every time you pass a Salvation Army collector.

204 ◆ Put white twinkle lights on your large house plants.

205 ◆ Have a special outfit or accessory that you wear only on Christmas day.

206 ◆ Regardless of the temperature, if you have a fireplace, have it blazing on Christmas Eve and Christmas Day.

207 ◆ Wrap a gift in an odd-shaped package so the recipient can't guess what it is.

208 ◆ If you have small children or pets, be careful when decorating with greenery that has poisonous leaves or berries, such as poinsettias, holly, and mistletoe.

209 ◆ Make a friend of an
enemy this Christmas.

210 ◆ On a clear night, find the bright North Star and recall the story of the Wise Men.

211 ◆ Teach children to look at the gift tag *before* they open the present so they will know whom to thank.

212 ◆ Don't burn wrapping paper in the fireplace. It's a fire and a health hazard.

213 ◆ Be a generous giver.

214 ◆ Be a gracious receiver.

215 ◆ Make it a daily practice during the Christmas season to do something nice for someone without telling them you did it.

216 ◆ Read "'Twas the Night Before Christmas" the night before Christmas.

217 ◆ Send Christmas cards with encouraging messages to military personnel on duty overseas.

218 ◆ Record your young child singing Christmas carols on a cassette tape. Send it to grandparents who live far away.

219 ◆ Be the first to lob a snowball and start a battle.

220 ◆ Set out a bowl of walnuts, brazils, and tangerines in the family room.

221 ◆ Buy a big red candle for the kitchen table. Light it every night at dinner during the holidays.

222 ◆ Attend a children's Christmas pageant.

223 ◆ Keep a fire extinguisher near the tree and in the kitchen.

224 ◆ Decorate your living room or family room with a pot of fragrant white narcissus.

225 ◆ Welcome a new family to your neighbourhood with a plate of Christmas goodies.

226 ◆ Never give a gift to someone else's child that you wouldn't want your own child to receive.

227 ◆ Open Christmas cards as a family activity each night at the dinner table. Read the messages aloud.

228 ◆ Give someone who's discouraged the gift of encouragement.

229 ◆ Make your family feel just as important as the company you have at Christmas.

230 ◆ Pay a debt for someone.

231 ◆ Add a new Christmas cassette or CD to your music collection each year.

232 ◆ Offer to carry someone's packages.

233 ◆ Plan a quiet evening with your family the week after Christmas. Talk about your goals for the coming year.

234 ◆ Take your family and some neighbourhood children ice skating.

## *235* ◆ *Brandy Butter for Christmas Pudding*

125g unsalted butter                    30-60ml brandy
175g icing sugar

Cream the butter until it's white. Gradually add the sugar and the brandy. Pipe or pile up into pyramid shape and then decorate with cherries. Place in the refrigerator for two hours, or until really hard.

   . . . or try this delicious alternative

## *Cumberland Rum Butter*

125g unsalted butter                    30-60ml rum
175g demerara sugar

Cream the butter until it's white. Gradually add the sugar and the rum. Pipe or pile up into a pyramid shape and then decorate with cherries. Place in the refrigerator for two hours, or until really hard.

236 ◆ Load the family in the car, slip in your favourite Christmas tape, and drive through the neighbourhood looking at the Christmas decorations. Roll down the windows and shout, "Merry Christmas" to everyone you see.

237 ◆ Anonymously send someone who's wronged you a Christmas card with a sincere wish for happiness and well-being.

238 ◆ Serve mince pies on a Santa Claus platter.

239 ◆ Give a small gift—such as a tree ornament—to each guest when you have a Christmas party.

240 ◆ If you're feeling harried, go to a church, sit in the sanctuary, and reflect on the real meaning of Christmas. You'll leave feeling more peaceful.

241 ◆ Host a Christmas reception for a friend who's started a new business.

242 ◆ Use festive postage stamps on envelopes and packages.

243 ◆ Consider taking a family trip one Christmas instead of exchanging gifts.

244 ◆ Introduce a shy person to others at the office Christmas party.

245 ◆ Toast your friends when they are in your home. Tell them how much it means to you to have them there.

246 ◆ Keep plenty of apple cider and microwave popcorn on hand for unexpected drop-in holiday guests.

247 ◆ Don't forget, no matter how many Christmas photos you take, next year you'll wish you had taken more.

248 ◆ Read to your family "The Gift of the Magi" by O. Henry.

249 ◆ This Christmas, write letters to several people who have had a positive influence on your life. Thank them for this gift they have given you.

250 ◆ Buy a book of Christmas carols and keep it open on the piano during the holidays.

251 ◆ Put Christmas lights and a small wreath on the dog kennel.

252 ◆ Let someone else have the parking space you've just found. Think of it as a gift to a stranger.

253 ◆ When travelling, pick up small inexpensive souvenir items that can be used as tree ornaments. They will remind you of your happy travels.

254 ◆ Ask the oldest married man and the youngest married woman to pull the Christmas turkey wishbone.

255 ◆ Give gifts with no strings attached.

256 ◆ Write with a red or green pen during the holidays.

257 ◆ Tie peppermints to children's packages.

258 ✦ Buy something from students holding a Christmas sale and tell them to keep the change.

259 ✦ Don't give an errand along with a gift. Unless you're certain of the correct size, don't give someone clothing. Exchanging clothes is a hassle.

260 ✦ Take a child to the library and take out a book of Christmas stories.

261 ◆ Keep money in individual envelopes to give spontaneously to others when you're touched by the Christmas spirit.

262 ◆ Write a Christmas greeting at the top of your business faxes.

263 ◆ When Christmas travels take you to cities where you have friends, call or write ahead and try to get together, even if it's for only a few minutes.

264 ◆ Include your children in the preparation of Christmas meals. This teaches them skills they will need in years to come.

265 ◆ Add a note of appreciation to the Christmas card you give your child's teacher.

266 ◆ This season, cut others—as well as yourself—more slack than usual.

267 ◆ Replace your shoelaces with a red one and a green one.

268 ◆ Invest in an inexpensive postal scale. It can save you time waiting in line at the post office.

269 ◆ Put pebbles inside children's gift boxes so that when they shake the packages, they won't be able to guess what's inside.

270 ♦ If your child gets a new game for Christmas, play it with him and let him win.

271 ♦ When you put away the decorations, label each box. You'll have a better chance of starting the season with joy next year.

272 ♦ Stop and help someone who's stuck in the snow.

273 ◆ Take a decorated miniature Christmas tree to someone in a hospital or a nursing home.

274 ◆ As a courtesy to your neighbours, alert them before you have a large Christmas party.

275 ◆ Be others-centered instead of self-centered. A person wrapped up in himself makes a very small package.

276 ◆ Take a walk with someone you love on Christmas afternoon.

277 ◆ Give tickets to a special Christmas performance to someone who couldn't otherwise afford to go.

278 ◆ Read *The Littlest Angel* by Charles Tazewell to a child.

279 ◆ Remember that the loving Christmas spirit in your home depends more on the words you speak than on the gifts you give.

280 ◆ If someone disappoints you this season, don't give a lecture. Give acceptance and forgiveness.

281 ◆ Once or twice, take a different route home from work and enjoy the decorations in another neighbourhood.

282 ◆ Turn off the lights and put on a recording of Bing Crosby's "White Christmas". Ask your spouse to dance.

283 ◆ Tour a historic home in your area that has been decorated for Christmas.

284 ◆ When you phone a store during the holidays, ask the clerk, "Are you with a customer or do you have time for me to ask you a question?"

285 ◆ Open Christmas gifts with your favourite Christmas music playing in the background.

286 ◆ Secretly shovel the snow off your neighbour's front path.

287 ◆ Answer your phone by saying, "Merry Christmas".

288 ◆ Throw orange or tangerine peels into your fire for a spicy aroma.

289 ◆ Write names and dates on the backs of Christmas photographs.

290 ◆ Pray that God will help you see opportunities to be a blessing to others this Christmas.

291 ◆ If you are having trouble deciding on gifts to give young nieces, nephews, and other youngsters on your list, ask friends who have children of the same sex and age for ideas.

292 ◆ Save the receipts for every gift you buy.

293 ◆ Learn the names of Santa's reindeer.

294 ◆ Learn the second verse to "Jingle Bells".

295 ◆ Challenge someone to sing all the verses of "The Twelve Days of Christmas".

296 ◆ Create a gag gift that is passed on to different family members every Christmas. A complimentary hotel shower cap always brings lots of laughs.

297 ◆ Use candles safely: (1) Don't leave burning candles unattended; (2) Be sure the candle is firmly anchored to its holder; (3) Use the right size or type of holder for the candle.

298 ◆ Have an extra ice scraper to give to someone who might need one.

299 ◆ Pay baby sitters a little extra during the Christmas season.

300 ◆ When a child mentions something that he or she would like to receive as a gift, never say, "We'll see", if you have no intention of getting it.

301 ◆ Order two take-out lunches—one for yourself and one to give to a homeless person.

302 ◆ Buy Christmas gifts from local artists and craftspeople.

303 ◆ When you have friends over and there's Christmas magic in the air, don't let the evening end early. Throw another log on the fire.

304 ◆ Offer to keep a friend's children when you learn that their sitter has cancelled right before a Christmas party.

305 ◆ Pay the toll for the car behind you during the week of Christmas.

306 ◆ Carry jumper cables. If you don't need them, you're set to help someone else.

307 ◆ Order and pay for a pizza for a neighbour. Ask the delivery person to tell them it's from Santa.

308 ◆ Set aside twenty minutes each day to catch your breath. Make yourself a cup of tea, put your feet up, and turn on the answering machine.

309 ◆ If you take a trip by plane during the holidays, offer to swap seats so a family can sit together.

310 ◆ Let someone with just a few items go ahead of you in line at the supermarket.

311 ◆ Use poster board and felt-tipped markers to create a giant-size family Christmas card for someone special.

312 ◆ If you're including young children in your Christmas open house, set up a separate area for them and enlist the help of a neighbourhood sixth former to supervise.

313 ◆ Get the conversation started around the Christmas dinner table by taking turns sharing "the Christmas I remember best", or "the craziest present I ever received".

314 ◆ Use package sealing tape—*not* string or twine— when sending packages. Tape won't get caught in machinery or conveyor belts.

315 ◆ Start a family tree-decorating tradition. Serve the same refreshments and play the same music every year.

316 ◆ At a Christmas buffet, offer to collect food for an older person.

317 ♦ When you hear the song "Rockin' Around the Christmas Tree", grab the family member closest to you and kick up your heels.

318 ♦ Offer to help a disabled person with his or her Christmas shopping.

319 ♦ This Christmas, give yourself the gift of living in peace with those things you cannot change.

320 ◆ If you have children who are old enough to wrap their own gifts, provide them with their own supply of wrapping materials.

321 ◆ Serve some meals in front of the fire.

322 ◆ If you don't have extended family close by, invite a family with similar circumstances to share some Christmas festivities with you.

323 ◆ Smile at police officers, fire fighters, emergency personnel, and security guards. Thank them for being on the job during the Christmas season.

324 ◆ Consider hosting a party the week after Christmas instead of trying to squeeze it in during the busy weeks before Christmas. Your house will still be decorated and it will be easier to relax and enjoy your guests.

325 ◆ Ask neighbours if you can watch their house, pick up their newspapers, and collect their mail when they are out of town during the holidays.

326 ◆ Let your child know you care about his or her world. Host a Christmas party for several school friends.

327 ◆ Give someone who's disappointed you the gift of a clean slate this Christmas.

328 ◆ Avoid misunderstandings during the holidays by trying to settle controversial family matters ahead of time.

329 ◆ During a long flight, offer to entertain a small child for a while for a parent travelling alone at Christmas.

330 ◆ Instead of wrapping packages, try putting gifts in decorative shopping bags filled with colourful tissue.

331 ◆ Christmas catalogues come earlier and earlier each year, but it's *never* too early to start ordering gifts and goodies.

332 ◆ Instead of giving gifts at the office, take up a collection to give to a designated charity.

333 ◆ Don't let a rude person steal your Christmas joy.

334 ◆ Give a pint of blood;
it's the gift of life.

335 ♦ If you are planning a large Christmas party, call early to reserve the equipment and supplies that need to be rented.

336 ♦ When you see a family or group taking pictures of each other, offer to take one of the whole group.

337 ♦ Give children toys that encourage their creativity.

338 ◆ Avoid fruitless shopping trips. Call stores before you leave home to check on prices and availability of the items you plan to buy.

339 ◆ Share baking with three friends. Each of you bake double batches of your favourite recipes; then swap.

340 ◆ Give your seat on the bus or train to someone holding lots of packages.

341 ◆ Let your children participate in decorating the house for Christmas. It's more important for them to help than for everything to look picture-perfect.

342 ◆ Don't purchase anything in a package that is damaged or looks as if it has been opened.

343 ◆ Acknowledge every gift you receive.

344 ◆ Write "Joy to the World" with your finger on a frosty window pane.

345 ◆ Follow the Irish tradition of putting a bird's nest in your Christmas tree.

346 ◆ Instead of buying expensive Christmas wrapping paper, purchase a large roll of plain white or brown kraft paper and a large roll of red plaid ribbon from a florist.

347 ◆ Sometimes students who live long distances away can't afford to go home for Christmas. Call the principal of a local college and ask if there might be a couple of students who would like to share a meal with your family.

348 ◆ If your office is at home, be realistic about how much you will be able to accomplish with the children out of school for Christmas.

## 349 ◆ Christmas Jelly

A delicious alternative for those who just can't face Christmas pudding.

---

**Yield: Serves 4 to 8 people (depending on appetites)**

---

~~125g seedless raisins~~
1 packet raspberry jelly
450g frozen raspberries (keep frozen)

30ml rum
225ml port
175g chopped walnuts

Soak the raisins overnight in the rum. Make the jelly with 150ml boiling water, stirring until dissolved. Add the port and cool but do not set. Put the fruit and nuts into a large glass serving bowl, or divide equally into 4 large or 6 small individual glasses. Pour over the cool jelly and leave to set. To make a richer dessert, serve with clotted cream.

350 ◆ For a quick Christmas centrepiece, fill a large bowl with red apples. Intersperse with sprigs of greenery.

351 ◆ Never prepare new recipes for Christmas meals unless you've tried them out at least once beforehand.

352 ◆ Serve cinnamon sticks with hot cider and peppermint sticks with hot chocolate.

353 ◆ Buy a children's Christmas music tape or CD. Listen and sing along with your children while you're running errands together in the car.

354 ◆ Make sure your car battery is in good condition. A dead battery in a car park challenges even the brightest Christmas spirit.

355 ◆ Let other cars pull in front of you.

356 ◆ Be sure to wave a thank you when somebody lets you into traffic.

357 ◆ If one family member lives far away and can't afford to travel home, suggest that other family members chip in and buy him a ticket.

358 ◆ Take time to remember that the greatest gift is a home filled with the people you love.

359 ◆ Volunteer to deliver Meals on Wheels to the house-bound.

360 ◆ Ask children, "What are you *giving* for Christmas?" instead of "What are you *getting* for Christmas?"

361 ◆ If you have friends who have lost family members since last Christmas, make a special effort to call and cheer them during the holidays.

362 ◆ Have a special Christmas tablecloth that's used only on Christmas Day.

363 ◆ Christmas entertaining doesn't have to be elaborate or complicated. Just make a big pot of chili, toss a green salad, and fry a pan of chips.

364 ◆ Watch The Morecambe and Wise Christmas Show.

365 ◆ Let younger children create their own Christmas wrapping paper with white paper and an assortment of rubber stamps and coloured ink pads.

366 ◆ Christmas is the season for time-honoured traditions. Don't attempt major changes.

367 ◆ Discover the quiet satisfaction of anonymous giving.

368 ◆ Avoid last-minute personal shopping. Decide ahead of time which clothes and accessories you will wear to Christmas festivities.

369 ◆ Keep your Christmas recipe collection in a special file or folder. Add to it each year.

370 ◆ Have a photo made of you and your family with Santa Claus.

371 ◆ Instead of exchanging gifts with close friends at Christmas, decide to take each other to lunch.

372 ◆ Take your camera to Christmas parties. Send the photos to your host or hostess with your thank-you note.

373 ◆ Make arrangements to donate leftover food from a Christmas party to a homeless shelter.

374 ◆ Save the original boxes for fragile Christmas decorations, so that you can pack them back securely after the holidays.

375 ◆ If you hide gifts, write down what you have hidden and where.

376 ◆ Keep up with the local news during the Christmas season to learn if there is someone who might need your help.

377 ◆ If you are taking a car trip with children during the holidays, create silly new verses for "The Twelve Days of Christmas".

378 ◆ As you pack up the Christmas tree decorations, ask family members to write a prediction for the coming year on a piece of paper. Put them in the ornament box and read them next year.

379 ◆ Don't try to do everything yourself. Remember, even Santa needs helpers.

380 ◆ Don't overplan your Christmas schedule. Leave a little room for spontaneity.

381 ◆ If you have young children, be sure to line up sitters well in advance for Christmas events.

382 ◆ When you put away your Christmas lights, wrap each string around a large empty gift box and slip a plastic bag over it.

383 ◆ The day you take down the Christmas decorations, hold a family council and ask everyone what they liked best and least about the holidays.

384 ◆ Put your name and address and the recipient's name and address inside the package as well as outside when sending out-of-town Christmas gifts. If the package is damaged, there will still be a way to ensure its delivery.

385 ◆ Use a heavy plastic waste bin to store bulky Christmas decorations.

386 ◆ Put stockings filled with small gifts and treats on the back of dining chairs for friends when they come to your home for a Christmas dinner.

387 ◆ When you are bidding your host good-bye at a Christmas party, don't linger at the door.

388 ◆ On the first of January, start a jar for loose pocket change. Save all year and use the money for a special family evening next Christmas.

389 ◆ Fill a pump-dispenser thermos with boiling water each morning as you're making breakfast. Then you'll be ready to fix a quick cup of instant cocoa or hot spiced tea for a drop-in guest.

390 ◆ Wrap a few small picture frames, fabric-covered blank books, or nonperishable food items for those you may have inadvertently left off your Christmas list. Put a blank gift tag on the package to be filled out later.

391 ◆ Make more space in your refrigerator for entertaining by temporarily transferring all the little bottles and jars into a picnic cooler.

392 ◆ Never wrap a gift in a box with a store's name on it unless the gift came from that store. It's confusing if the gift needs to be returned.

393 ◆ Save your gift lists from year to year. This will help avoid duplications and give you ideas for next year.

394 ◆ Keep all packing cartons in case you need to make returns.

395 ◆ When sending Christmas thank-you notes, tuck in a snapshot of yourself enjoying the gift.

396 ◆ Try to have Christmas thank-you notes written and posted by January 15.

397 ◆ End an evening spent with family and close friends by forming a circle, holding hands, and singing a favourite Christmas carol.

398 ◆ If your children are grown up, offer to take one of your friend's small children out for a special Christmas activity.

399 ◆ Research your family history and serve a special Christmas food or drink that your ancestors might have enjoyed.

400 ◆ Amidst the hustle and bustle, the stress and the strain, take time to be good to yourself.

401 ◆ If you can't fit all your guests at one table for Christmas dinner, set up a second table in another room and have them exchange places between dinner and dessert.

402 ◆ Let the youngest child in the family who's old enough read the Christmas story on Christmas Eve. Record it on tape, and save it for them when they are grown up.

403 ◆ Every year, buy a tree ornament for each of your children. Choose ones that represent important events that happened to them during the past year. When they move away from home, give them their collection of ornaments to put on their own tree.

404 ◆ Don't overwhelm youngsters by allowing them to open lots of presents in a short amount of time.

## *405 ◆ Savoury Baked Apricots*

This is delicious with any traditional Christmas meal: turkey, ham, or goose. People always come back for seconds, so be sure to make plenty!

---

**Yield: 8 servings    Oven: 150°C/300°F or Gas Mark 2**

---

2 500g cans apricot halves, drained
1 450g can tart cherries, drained
225g brown sugar

225g Ritz crackers
50g butter

Line a baking dish with 1 can of apricot halves and sprinkle a quarter of the brown sugar over them. Add a quarter of the crumbled Ritz crackers and dot with a quarter of the butter, cut into chunks. Next, add half the cherries, followed by another quarter of the brown sugar, Ritz crackers, and butter. Make another layer with the second can of apricot halves, a quarter of the brown sugar, crumbled Ritz crackers, and butter. Finish with the remaining cherries, brown sugar, Ritz crackers, and butter. Bake for 1 hour.

406 ◆ Offer to hide your neighbours' Christmas gifts for their children so that young snoopers won't discover them.

407 ◆ Post warranty cards promptly.

408 ◆ Hang up stockings for every member of the family. Don't forget the pets.

409 ◆ Watch the television special, "A Charlie Brown Christmas".

410 ◆ Send your Sunday school teacher a Christmas card and a note of appreciation.

411 ◆ For toys and appliances, save manufacturers' addresses, consumer-service information, and hotline numbers.

412 ◆ Everyone loves a teddy bear. Give at least one every Christmas.

413 ◆ Remember that peace on earth starts with peace in our homes and in our hearts.

414 ◆ Take your children with you when you make a cash donation to a homeless shelter or charity, and let them experience the joy of giving.

415 ◆ Don't use the words "I'm on a diet" during the Christmas season.

416 ◆ After opening the presents, hug all your family members and tell them they are the best gift of all.

417 ◆ The week after Christmas, help your children go through their toys and select some that are still in good condition to give to the less fortunate.

418 ◆ Never miss an opportunity to shake hands with Santa Claus.

419 ◆ If your family doesn't celebrate many Christmas traditions, let this be the year you create some.

420 ◆ For Christmas dinner, prepare as many do-ahead dishes as you can.

421 ◆ Turn down your thermostat before the guests arrive for a large Christmas get-together. Crowded rooms heat up quickly.

422 ◆ Stock up on candles, Christmas cards, tree decorations, and paper goods at after-Christmas sales.

423 ◆ Feed someone's expired parking meter.

424 ◆ Don't expect your husband or wife to wear a halo during the holidays. Give your spouse the gift of patience, flexibility, and a sense of humour.

425 ◆ On New Year's Day, light three candles and think about the three things that happened the past year for which you are most thankful.

426 ◆ In addition to your regular Christmas card list, track down the addresses of a couple of people with whom you've lost touch and send them a Christmas greeting.

427 ◆ Save a length of Christmas tree trunk to burn as next year's yule log.

428 ◆ Look the other way when Granny and Granddad spoil your children.

429 ◆ Don't forget to put out Santa's sherry and mince pies.

430 ◆ Don't forget to hang the mistletoe.

431 ◆ Don't forget the batteries.

432 ◆ Don't forget whose birthday we're celebrating.

*Dear Reader:*

If you would like to share a couple of your
favourite family traditions or Christmas ideas with us,
we'd love to hear from you.
Our address is:

CHRISTMAS JOYS
P.O. Box 150285
Nashville, TN 37215
U.S.A.